W9-CLV-425

EXPLORING SCIENCE

HUMAN BODY SYSTEMS

MAINTAINING THE BODY'S FUNCTIONS

BY SHARON KATZ COOPER

Content Adviser: Debra Carlson, Ph.D., Associate Professor
Normandale Community College, Bloomington, Minnesota

Science Adviser: Terrence E. Young Jr., M.Ed., M.L.S.,
Jefferson Parish (Louisiana) Public School System

Reading Adviser: Rosemary G. Palmer, Ph.D., Department of Literacy,
College of Education, Boise State University

 Compass Point Books · Minneapolis, Minnesota

Compass Point Books • 3109 West 50th Street, #115 • Minneapolis, MN 55410

Visit Compass Point Books on the Internet at *www.compasspointbooks.com*
or e-mail your request to *custserv@compasspointbooks.com*

Photographs ©: Manfred Kage/Peter Arnold, Inc., cover; AFP/Getty Images, 4,17,38; Alfred Pasieka/
Photo Researchers, Inc., 5,12; Eye of Science, Science Photo Library, 6; David Scharf/Peter Arnold,
Inc., 7, 24; Phil Degginger/Bruce Coleman Inc., 9; Ed Reschke/Peter Arnold, Inc., 13, 15; Dr.
Dennis Kunkel/Visuals Unlimited, 14; Geoffrey Stewart/The Medical File/Peter Arnold. Inc., 18;
Arthur Glauberman/Photo Researchers, Inc., 19; BSIP, Kokel/Science Photo Library, 20; Lester
V. Bergman/Corbis, 22; Steve Allan/Peter Arnold, Inc., 23; Shutterstock/Rachel B. Krech, 25;
BSIP, Lenee/Science Photo Library, 26; Anatomical Travelogue/Photo Researchers, Inc., 27, 33;
Biology Media/Science Photo Library, 30; Visuals Unlimited/Corbis, 31; The Granger Collection,
New York, 32; Science Photo Library/Photo Researchers, Inc., 36; SIU/Peter Arnold, Inc., 42;
Jochen Tack/Peter Arnold, Inc., 43; Mehau Kulyk/Photo Researchers, Inc., 44; Gregory K.
Scott/PhotoResearchers, Inc., 46.

Editor: **Anthony Wacholtz**
Page Production: Bobbie Nuytten
Photo Researcher: Lori Bye
Illustrators: Eric Hoffmann and Farhana Hossain

Art Director: Jaime Martens
Creative Director: Keith Griffin
Editorial Director: Carol Jones
Managing Editor: Catherine Neitge

Library of Congress Cataloging-in-Publication Data
Cooper, Sharon Katz.
   Human body systems : maintaining the body's functions / by Sharon Katz Cooper.
      p. cm. – (Exploring science)
   Includes index.
   ISBN-13: 978-0-7565-1958-2 (library binding)
   ISBN-10: 0-7565-1958-6 (library binding)
   ISBN-13: 978-0-7565-1964-3 (paperback)
   ISBN-10: 0-7565-1964-0 (paperback)
   1. Human physiology–Juvenile literature. I. Title. II. Series.
   QP37C789 2007
   612–dc22   2006027046

(About the Author)

Sharon Katz Cooper is a writer and science educator. She enjoys
writing about science and social studies topics for children and
young adults. She lives in Fairfax, Virginia, with her husband, Jason,
and son, Reuven.

TABLE OF CONTENTS

c h a p t e r   *p a g e*

1 ONE BODY, MANY SYSTEMS 4

2 SUPPORT SYSTEMS 6

3 COMMUNICATING WITH THE BODY 15

4 TRANSPORTATION AND PROTECTION 23

5 OBTAINING ENERGY AND GETTING RID OF WASTE 33

6 INTO THE FUTURE 38

Glossary 45

Did You Know? 46

Further Resources 47

Index 48

One Body, Many Systems

A YOGA INSTRUCTOR takes a deep breath and slowly lets it out. A runner flexes his ankles and moves his feet around in a circle before a race. A student, deep in thought, concentrates while taking an exam. Each of these actions uses one or more of

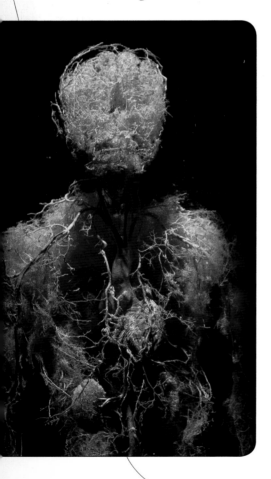

the body's major systems. Like all animals, humans have several different systems to help their bodies live and function. There are 11 major systems that carry out the body's activities—skin, skeletal, muscular, nervous, endocrine, circulatory, respiratory, immune, digestive, urinary, and reproductive. Each system has a specific and essential job to do.

Together, these systems keep the body running smoothly and completing all the tasks required to live. For example, many systems are used when you run. First of all, you need a lot of energy before you start. This energy comes from your digestive system, which takes in food and

The heart and blood vessels of the circulatory system control blood flow throughout the human body.

processes it into a form the body's cells can use.

Once you are ready to go, your nervous system sends messages from your brain throughout your body to tell it to move. Your muscular system receives these messages and begins to push and pull your bones to move in the right direction.

The brain also sends messages to the circulatory system to increase the blood flow to and from the heart. As you speed up, your respiratory system brings in more oxygen and releases carbon

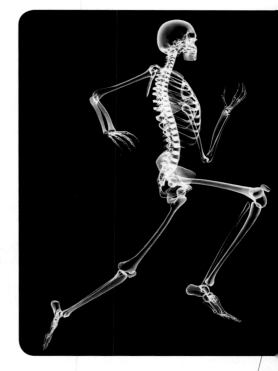

dioxide faster, allowing you to breathe more quickly. While you are racing forward, your skin sweats out extra moisture to keep your body cool as you heat up. Throughout the run, the skeletal system helps support the body and maintain balance.

Without any one of these systems, an important job would go undone. Understanding how these systems work together helps us learn more about what the body needs and how it functions.

Especially during physical activity like running, the bones of the skeletal system provide a structure that supports the human body.

CHAPTER TWO

⊕ **Support Systems**

IN ORDER TO MOVE, you need skin, bones, and muscles. These three systems—the skin, skeletal system, and muscular system—also protect and support the body.

THE MANY FUNCTIONS OF SKIN

The internal organs of humans must be protected and must maintain constant moisture and temperature levels. The skin helps to do both of these things. Skin is made up of two main layers, the epidermis and the dermis. The epidermis is the part that you see.

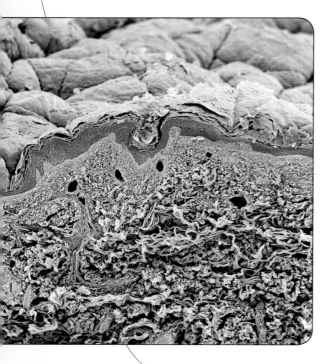

The topmost portion of the epidermis is made up of many layers of flat, dead cells that the body constantly sheds. These dead outer cells contain a waterproof substance called keratin that helps protect the underlying layers of cells.

Under those dead epidermal cells are living cells that are always dividing and

Dead skin cells (tan) are constantly shed and are replaced by the epidermal cells (red). Underneath the epidermis is the dermis (brown), which supports and nourishes the epidermis.

replacing the dead ones. These cells contain melanin, a substance that gives skin its color and protects it from the strong rays of the sun.

Underneath the epidermis lies the dermis, the thicker inner layer of skin. Like the epidermis, it is thicker on some parts of the body than others. For example, the dermis is thicker on a person's back than it is on the eyelids. The dermis contains blood vessels, nerves, and sweat and oil glands.

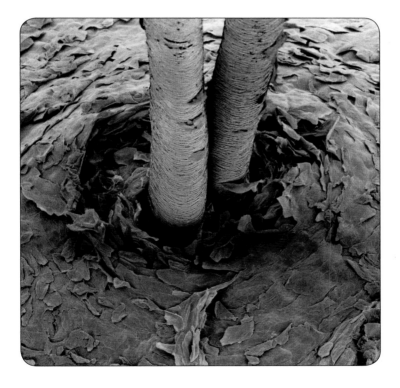

The skin around hair follicles magnified 320 times

Skin helps maintain body temperature. When the body heats up, tiny blood vessels in the skin expand so that more blood can flow through them. This expansion creates more surface area. With more surface area, the body releases heat through radiation, cooling the body. On the other hand, if the body's temperature gets too low, the blood vessels contract to minimize heat loss and warm the body. Another way that skin cools the body is by sweating. When you sweat, your skin gets wet. As the sweat evaporates, your body cools.

Skin also serves to protect the body against an invasion of dangerous germs that can cause disease. Most of these microbes land on the skin, which is the body's first line of defense. Healthy skin stops the microbes before they ever enter the body so they cannot cause much damage. If the microbes invade the body, however, they can do much more harm.

SUPPORT STRUCTURE

Feel the side of your index finger. The hard material you are feeling is one of three bones in your finger. Even though they are hard, bones are made of living tissue that grows and changes throughout your life.

The adult human skeleton has 206 bones and is made up of two major parts. One part is called the axial skeleton,

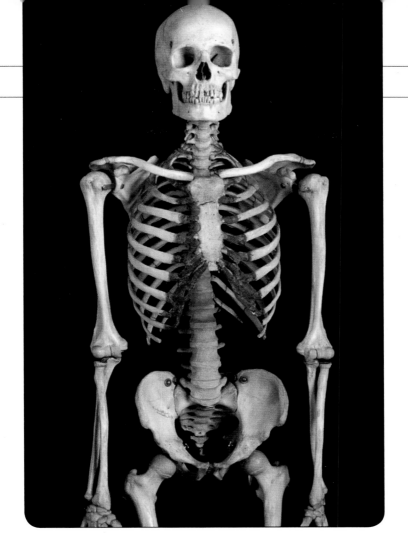

which includes the skull, ribs, sternum, and vertebrae—the bones protecting the spinal cord. The other part is the appendicular skeleton, which mainly includes the bones of the arms and legs. Like a building's steel structure, the skeletal system serves as a secure framework to protect all the tissues and organs of the body.

Donated skeletons are used by the science and medical fields so students can study the bones firsthand.

HUMAN SKELETON

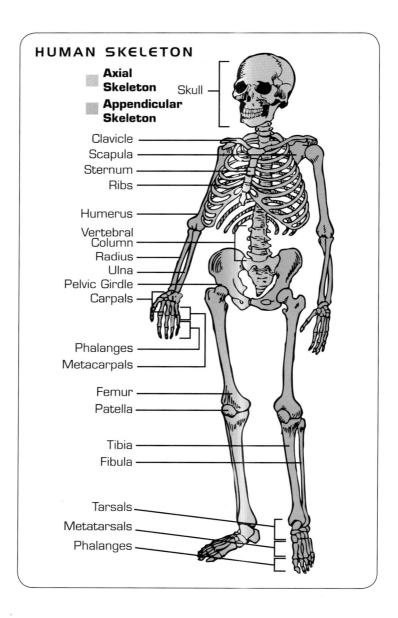

■ **Axial Skeleton**

■ **Appendicular Skeleton**

Skull

Clavicle
Scapula
Sternum
Ribs

Humerus

Vertebral Column
Radius
Ulna
Pelvic Girdle
Carpals

Phalanges
Metacarpals

Femur
Patella

Tibia
Fibula

Tarsals
Metatarsals
Phalanges

DID YOU KNOW?

Children have about 300 bones—nearly 100 more than adults. Some bones, especially those in the skull, fuse together during development.

In addition, the skeleton helps the body move efficiently. Movement is possible at joints, where two or more bones meet. There are many joints in the body, like those in elbows and knees. These joints are held together by ligaments, which are bands of tough tissue.

The ends of bones are covered with cartilage, a softer substance that helps bones move smoothly. Between some bones is a fluid-filled sac that helps absorb the shock of movement. These sacs can sometimes be found between bones and skin as well.

Inside some bones is a substance called marrow that produces red blood cells, white blood cells, and platelets for the circulatory system. Bones are also storage units. Minerals like calcium and phosphorus are stored in bones until they are needed.

Osteoporosis

Osteoporosis is a disease of the bones. A person with this painful disease has brittle, fragile bones that are easily broken. Bones become weak because of a loss of calcium and other minerals. From the time a person is born until the age of 30, the bones grow in weight and density, fueled by a proper diet and regular exercise. After the age of 30, bone tissue begins to deteriorate faster than the body can replace it. If the body has not stored enough calcium, the person could develop osteoporosis. The result is broken bones, particularly in the spine, hips, and wrists.

The best way to prevent osteoporosis is to eat a well-balanced diet with a lot of calcium throughout your lifetime. It is also important to exercise regularly, with emphasis on weight-bearing activities, such as walking, running, and lifting weights.

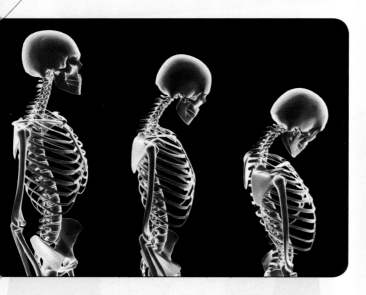

A stooped posture is one of the warning signs of osteoporosis. The hunched appearance is the result of an extreme curvature of the spine, which is caused by bone deterioration.

MUSCLING IN

The muscular system is important for movement and strength. There are three kinds of muscles—smooth, cardiac, and skeletal.

Smooth muscles are sheets of cells found in the walls of blood vessels and hollow organs of the digestive, respiratory, urinary, and reproductive tracts. Smooth muscle is used to squeeze. You do not voluntarily control smooth muscle; your brain controls it without your attention.

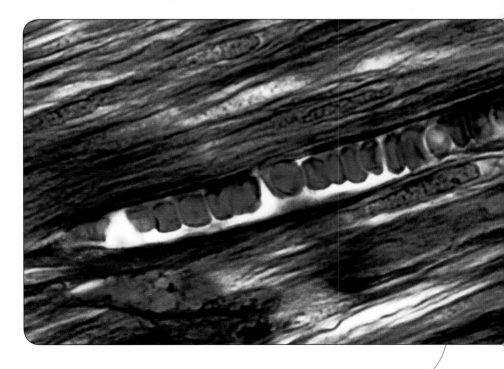

A line of red blood cells in a smooth muscle magnified 500 times

Cardiac muscles are only found in the heart. They form a network that helps the heart to work efficiently. These muscles' only function is to help the heart keep up its regular pattern of pumping blood—the heartbeat.

Skeletal muscles are attached to bones. They work with the tendons, cords of tissue that attach muscles to bones. When skeletal muscles pull to move the body, they tug on the tendons, making the bone move in the direction you want to go. Skeletal muscles are voluntary muscles, which means they can be consciously controlled. They are used when running, walking, talking, or chewing.

The individual fibers of a skeletal muscle can be easily seen when magnified 600 times.

Communicating with the Body

IF YOU HAVE EVER played a video game, you know that it requires you to make decisions very quickly based on constantly changing information. Your senses gather information, which needs to be processed to determine what you will do next. The nervous system allows you to interpret and respond to the information you receive from your senses.

THE CONTROL CENTER

The nervous system is mostly made up of basic units called neurons. Neurons are specialized cells that transmit information in the form of tiny electrical impulses from one part of the body to another.

There are three kinds of neurons—sensory neurons, inter-neurons, and motor neurons. Sensory neurons carry nerve impulses from receptors in the senses and send them to the brain and spinal cord. For example, these neurons transmit impulses about bright light that enters the eyes or about smooth-

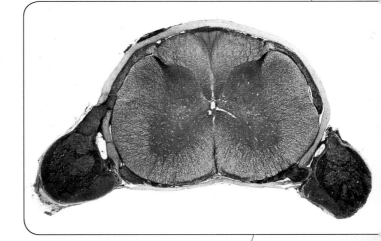

The spinal cord is encased in the vertebal column for protection.

muscle contractions in the stomach. Interneurons inside the brain and spinal cord process the incoming information. Motor neurons transmit responses to the information in the form of additional nerve impulses from the brain and spinal cord to other parts of the body.

The nervous system is broken down into the central and peripheral nervous systems. The brain and spinal cord make up the central nervous system and operate as the body's control center. The peripheral nervous system is composed of nerves that connect the central nervous system to the rest of the body. These two systems work together to coordinate all of the body's activities.

The brain and spinal cord process all of the incoming information. The brain also controls all the systems of the body. Lungs fill with air, a stomach processes food, and a body continues to grow because of the brain.

The brain has several sections, but there are three main sections that control the majority of the body's functions—the brain stem, the cerebellum, and the cerebrum. The brain stem

DID YOU KNOW?

The human brain weighs about 3 pounds (1.4 kilograms), which is about 2 percent of an average human's body weight.

controls involuntary activities, which do not require conscious thought to occur. These activities include regulating the heart rate and breathing. The cerebellum controls balance, posture, and coordination. The cerebrum interprets information gathered from the senses and controls voluntary activities.

Within the cerebrum, there are four lobes—frontal, parietal, temporal, and occipital. The frontal lobe starts the process of voluntary skeletal muscle movements throughout the body. The parietal lobe controls interpretation of information

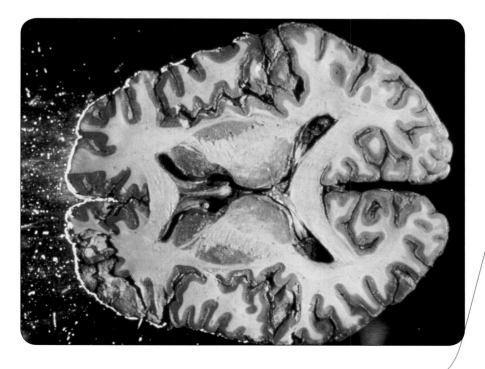

A cross-section of a human brain, revealing much of the cerebrum

from the skin, such as heat, cold, and pain. The temporal lobe interprets sounds, while the occipital lobe interprets vision.

Despite this current knowledge of the lobes, scientists still do not know a lot about how the cerebrum works. The cerebrum is where we assemble information, formulate reason, and develop intelligence and personality. It is what makes each person unique.

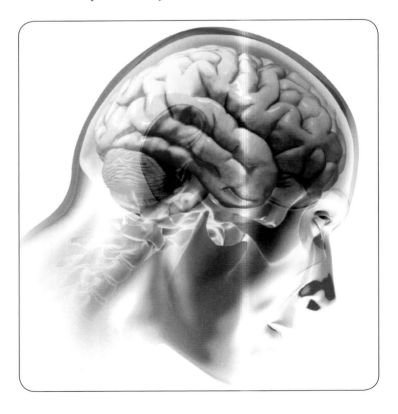

The cerebrum is made up four lobes—frontal (pink), parietal (green), temporal (purple), and occipital (orange). The cerebellum (brown) is located underneath the cerebrum.

Brain Injury

Scientists are still working to unlock the mysteries of the brain. Since the brain controls the entire body, injuries to the brain affect behavior, memory, and the ability to perform normal tasks. Different parts of the brain control specific functions, so the kind of difficulty a person has after a brain injury depends on where the injury has occurred. By observing various kinds of brain injuries, doctors have gained insight into how the brain works.

For example, if the cerebellum is injured, muscle movements may become jerky. If the temporal lobes are damaged, a person may have difficulty understanding spoken words or other sounds. Damage to the parietal lobes may result in difficulty naming objects and writing words, while damage to the frontal lobes can limit a person's ability to speak clearly.

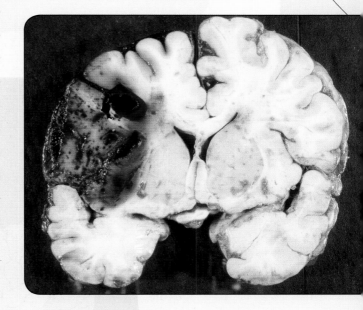

Bleeding in the brain tissue, known as cerebral hemorrhaging, is one type of brain injury.

A large part of the brain's work is bringing together information gathered by the senses and trying to decide what to do with it. Senses are important extensions of the nervous system.

Sound is created by vibrations called sound waves. The eardrum, middle ear, and inner ear detect these waves and transmit that information to the brain as a nerve impulse, allowing us to hear. Touch works in a similar way. The skin feels a

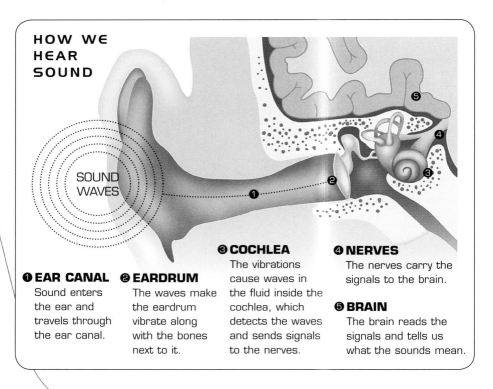

HOW WE HEAR SOUND

SOUND WAVES

❶ EAR CANAL
Sound enters the ear and travels through the ear canal.

❷ EARDRUM
The waves make the eardrum vibrate along with the bones next to it.

❸ COCHLEA
The vibrations cause waves in the fluid inside the cochlea, which detects the waves and sends signals to the nerves.

❹ NERVES
The nerves carry the signals to the brain.

❺ BRAIN
The brain reads the signals and tells us what the sounds mean.

physical stimulus, like pressure, heat, or pain, which becomes a nerve impulse that is sent to the brain. Some parts of the skin have more receptors than others. The areas with the greatest numbers of touch receptors are those we think of as most sensitive—fingertips, eyelids, lips, tongue, and hands.

The senses of taste and smell use sensitive receptors in the body that react to chemicals in food or other substances and send impulses to the brain. The brain then interprets what something smells or tastes like.

Sight involves the brain's understanding of light and dark. In the back of the eye is a thin layer of nerve tissue called the retina. The retina's cells are very sensitive to light. When light hits these cells, impulses in the optic nerves send this information to the brain. The brain translates that information into images that allow you to understand what you see.

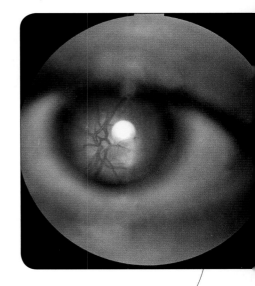

MESSENGER'S ASSISTANT

In addition to the nervous system, there is another system that sends messages throughout the body. The endocrine system is composed of the cells, tissues,

The blood vessels in the retina (orange) are visible through the lens of an optical instrument.

and organs that secrete hormones used in different parts of the body. They play an important role in regulating metabolism, growth, and reproduction.

Many hormones are produced in the hypothalamus, a part of the brain that regulates several of the body's functions. These hormones travel through the blood to the pituitary gland, which is a group of hormone-producing cells connected to the brain. These hormones tell the pituitary gland to speed up or slow down the cycle of hormone production. For example, an increase in the production of testosterone in teenage boys or estrogen in teenage girls leads to the onset of puberty.

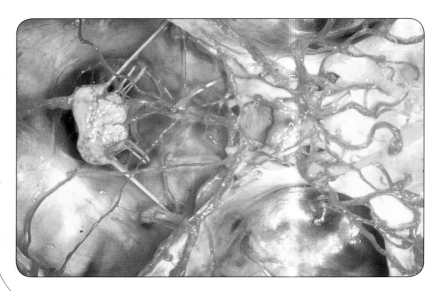

The pituitary gland is a powerhouse for producing essential hormones for the body.

Transportation and Protection

BLOOD TRANSPORTS NUTRIENTS and fluids to all parts of the body. The heart and the network of blood vessels that provide this transportation is called the circulatory system.

Blood is made up of four components: red blood cells, white blood cells, platelets, and plasma. Red blood cells are disc-shaped. Their job is to carry oxygen to the body's cells. White blood cells are spherical and help fight infections and disease. White blood cells make up less than 1 percent of your blood. Platelets are cell fragments that help blood clot, or stop bleeding, after an injury. Plasma is the liquid part of blood that makes up more than half of its volume. It is pale yellow and carries the other three blood components through the body's blood vessels.

There are five types of blood vessels that transport blood to all of the body's parts: arteries, arterioles, capillaries, venules, and veins. Arteries are

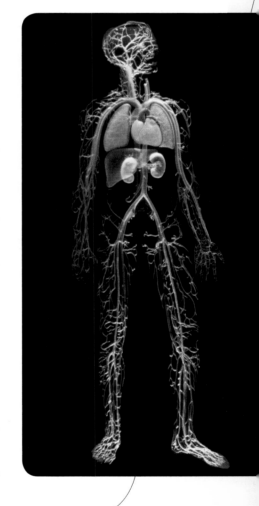

Blood vessels branch out to all parts of the body.

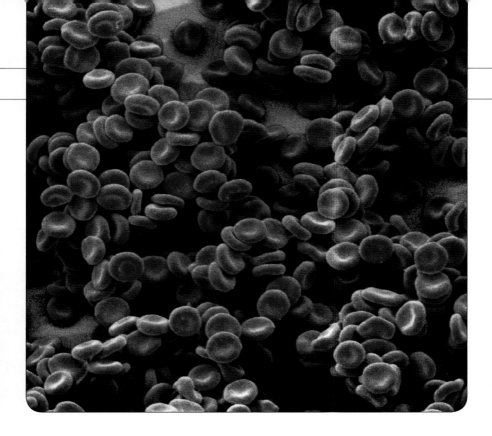

large, muscular vessels that carry oxygen-rich blood from the heart. The arteries branch into smaller blood vessels called arterioles. The arterioles branch out until they become capillaries, the tiniest blood vessels of all. Capillaries are so small that they allow nutrients and gases to move directly from the blood into the tissues, which are groups of cells working together to do a particular job. When blood leaves the tissues, it flows into tiny venules, which eventually become veins. Veins carry oxygen-poor blood from the tissues and organs back to the heart and lungs. The blood then releases carbon dioxide into the lungs and picks up more oxygen to circulate through the body again.

If you stacked 100 red blood cells on top of each other, they would equal the thickness of a dime.

The heart is the center of the circulatory system. It is a large, strong muscle that keeps blood flowing continuously throughout the body. Each time the heart beats, blood flows through its chambers and out into blood vessels. The force of blood flow against the inner walls of arteries is called blood pressure. Blood pressure rises and falls as the heart contracts and relaxes, creating a pulse.

The human heart pumps 1,900 gallons (7,200 liters) of blood in a single day.

Blood Donation

A person involved in a serious accident or needing surgery may require additional blood to replace the blood that was lost. Every year, thousands of people donate blood so that others may have it in emergencies. A regular blood donation is about 1 pint (.5 liters). The body replaces that blood in about a month, so some people are regular donors. About 32,000 pints (15,000 liters) of donated blood are used each year in the United States.

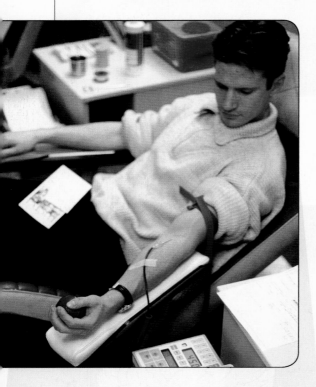

There are four main blood types: A, B, AB, and O. Doctors have to be very careful about what kind of blood they give to the people who need it. If they transfer the wrong kind of blood, the body will reject it. Doctors can give A blood to people with A or AB blood, and they can give B blood to people with B or AB blood. AB blood can only be given to others with AB blood, while O can be given to anybody.

According to the American Red Cross, only 5 percent of the U.S. population donates blood each year.

BREATHING IN AND OUT

One of the most important functions of the respiratory system is to provide oxygen to the organs and systems of the body. It also is responsible for removing carbon dioxide from the body. It works with the circulatory system, using blood as the transportation system for oxygen and carbon dioxide.

The respiratory system consists of the lungs, airways, and the diaphragm. When you inhale, air rushes through your nose or mouth and travels down a tube called the trachea, which leads to the lungs. The trachea divides into smaller tubes called bronchi. The trachea and bronchi are lined with tiny cilia and mucus that trap most of the tiny particles of dirt that come in with air.

The bronchi branch into smaller bronchioles, which then branch into even smaller airways in the lungs. Eventually, these airways lead to thousands of tiny sacs called alveoli. The walls of the alveoli are only one cell thick, which makes it possible for the exchange of oxygen and

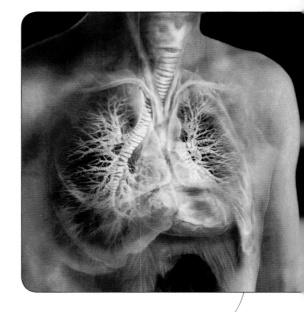

The respiratory system is like an upside-down tree, with the trachea making up the trunk and the bronchi and bronchioles making up the branches.

carbon dioxide. Used blood arrives in the alveoli and diffuses its carbon dioxide, which is then transported out of the body. At the same time, blood receives new oxygen. The refreshed blood can then leave the lungs and transport its new supply of oxygen throughout the body.

The diaphragm and muscles between the ribs aid in breathing by drawing air into the lungs and forcing it out. The alveoli inflate like tiny balloons during inhalation, and they

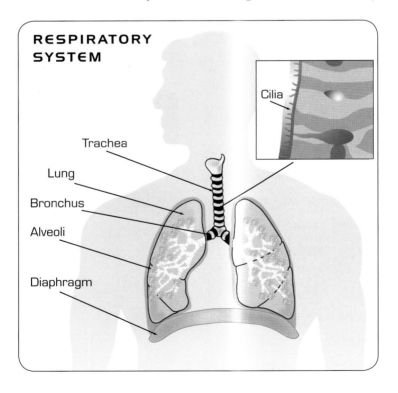

RESPIRATORY SYSTEM

Cilia

Trachea

Lung

Bronchus

Alveoli

Diaphragm

deflate slightly during exhalation. Breathing is involuntarily controlled by the brain stem. When you are excited or exercising, your brain senses a greater need for oxygen, and you will breathe more quickly.

PROTECTION FROM DISEASE

When you are sick and have a high temperature or a stuffy nose, your body is fighting a disease. The system that fights off disease is the immune system.

The skin is the first line of defense against disease. Skin is made of densely packed cells that prevent many disease-causing microbes from entering your body. Skin is also covered with mucus, sweat, and saliva, which trap microbes and often kill them. Some microbes manage to get through the skin's defenses, mainly through the mouth and nose. Once this happens, the body's immune system takes over. There are several kinds of white blood cells, and they fight diseases in different ways.

DID YOU KNOW?

The human immunodeficiency virus (HIV), which can lead to AIDS, attacks the immune system directly by destroying the cells that help to produce antibodies.

When microbes enter the body, white blood cells called phagocytes travel through the circulatory system to the infected area. There they surround and destroy the microbes. As phagocytes do their job, they cause the body's temperature to go up, and the person develops a fever. A fever is actually a positive symptom for fighting disease because many microbes cannot survive in higher temperatures. Fever also speeds up some of the body's processes, helping it to heal itself more quickly.

After a few days, the body's immune system may develop antibodies to defend against the specific microbe. This specific defense is called immunity. Once your body has been infected with a specific kind of disease and develops antibodies to it,

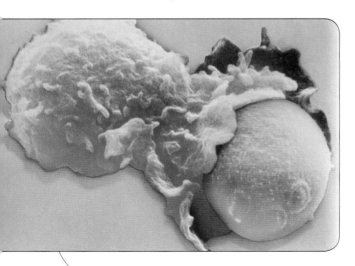

your immune system will recognize the same infection in the future.

Doctors have used this knowledge to create vaccines, which are weakened or harmless forms of a microbe. An injection of a vaccine

White blood cells work hard to engulf and destroy microbes that invade the body.

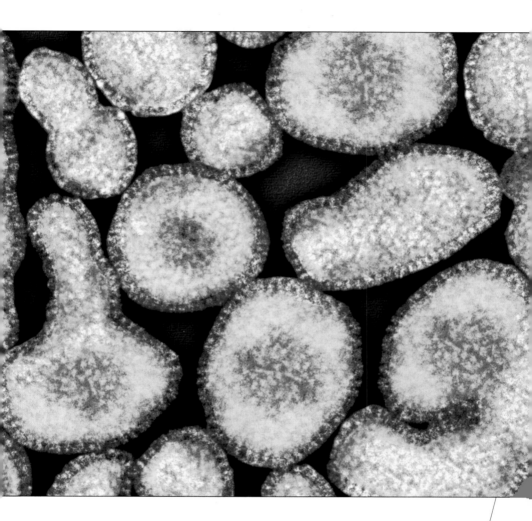

causes the body to produce antibodies and become immune to that microbe's disease. Once that happens, it is unlikely that the person will become sick from that particular disease.

Influenza type A is a very contagious virus that can spread rapidly from person to person.

Discovery of Vaccinations

In the late 1700s, a doctor in England named Edward Jenner came up with the idea of creating a vaccine. He observed workers in his dairy who got cowpox disease from their cows. He noticed that the same workers did not seem to get smallpox, a deadly disease that was common during that time.

To test his theory, in 1796 Jenner intentionally infected an 8-year-old child with cowpox. The boy developed a mild case of the disease. Several weeks later, Jenner exposed him to smallpox, yet the boy remained healthy. Because the two diseases are very similar, the boy's immune system had developed cowpox antibodies that also prevented smallpox.

Edward Jenner (1749–1823)

Obtaining Energy and Getting Rid of Waste

THE DIGESTIVE SYSTEM is the group of organs that processes food and breaks it down into fuel the body can use. This system takes in food, digests it, and forces it along the digestive tract. Special organs absorb the nutrients from the food and transport them to the circulatory system.

The digestive system is a long and winding tube that runs through the middle of the body, from the mouth to the anus. Each part of the tube has a special shape and function. From the time a piece of food enters the mouth to the time it exits the anus, it has traveled about 30 feet (9 meters).

The digestive process starts in the mouth. When food is chewed, the tongue helps to move the food around in the mouth. The grinding movement of the teeth breaks the food down into pieces small enough to swallow, and the saliva begins to chemically digest the food molecules. Once

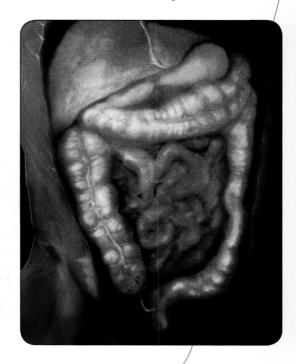

The digestive system processes food for nutrients that keep the body healthy.

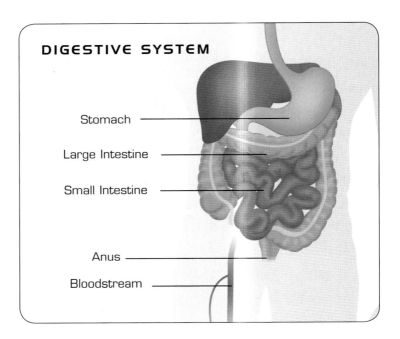

DIGESTIVE SYSTEM

Stomach

Large Intestine

Small Intestine

Anus

Bloodstream

the food is swallowed, it passes through the pharynx and enters the esophagus. Muscles in the esophagus push the food down to its bottom, where the food enters the stomach. In the stomach, muscles mix the food with digestive juices made of acids and enzymes to further break it down.

The stomach slowly releases chyme, which is partially digested food, into the small intestine. The small intestine, which is about 20 feet (6 m) long and 1 inch (2.5 centimeters) in diameter, moves the digested food by contracting its smooth muscle. As the chyme moves, it passes over thousands

Balanced Nutrition

The body needs six kinds of nutrients to function: carbohydrates, fats, proteins, minerals, vitamins, and water. These nutrients come from the food you eat and the fluids you drink. Carbohydrates provide the body with quick energy, while fats build cells, produce hormones, protect the body from injury, and insulate it against cold. Proteins are also used to make building materials and hormones, as well as enzymes and antibodies.

The body needs minerals like iron and calcium to build bones and teeth, help the red blood cells carry oxygen, and transmit nerve impulses. Vitamins regulate processes in the body, such as metabolism, blood clotting, and formation of red blood cells. Water makes up about 75 percent of your body. It is necessary for most of the body's functions.

NUTRIENTS THE BODY NEEDS

Nutrient	Foods Found In	Most Important Benefit
Carbohydrates	Bread, pasta, potatoes	Obtains energy
Fats	Meat, nuts, oils	Stores energy
Proteins	Fish, poultry, beans	Enhances muscles
Iron	Liver, leafy vegetables	Transports and stores oxygen
Calcium	Milk, cheese	Maintains strong teeth and bones
Vitamin A	Broccoli, tomatoes	Regulates growth
Vitamin C	Fruit, leafy vegetables	Aids in healing
B Vitamins	Meat, nuts, yogurt	Creates red blood cells

It is important to eat a variety of foods in order to receive all of the nutrients necessary for a healthy body.

of villi—tiny projections that line the intestine. The villi absorb the nutrients from the chyme and transfer them into the blood for transportation to all of the body's cells.

By the time the chyme travels through the small intestine, most of the material that is left cannot be digested. This waste material moves into the large intestine, which is about 5 feet (1.5 m) long and 2 ½ inches (6.5 cm) in diameter. The walls of the large intestine absorb water from the waste so it can be reused in the body. Bacteria in the large intestine make vitamins that the body can use. By the time the material has reached the end of the large intestine, it is much more solid.

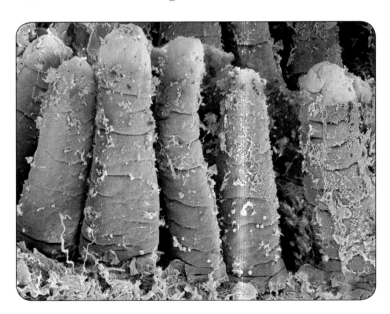

Villi trap food particles as they move through the small intestine.

What is left is not of much use to the body, so it is eliminated through the anus.

GETTING RID OF WASTE

The urinary system works alongside the digestive system, filtering blood and producing a waste fluid called urine. The urinary system consists of two kidneys, a bladder, two ureters—which are tubes connecting the kidneys to the bladder—and the urethra. The kidneys filter the blood and take most of the liquid and nutrients back for the body to reuse. The remaining fluid, urine, is then sent down the ureters, where it enters the bladder, an expandable sac that collects the urine. The urethra is the small tube from the bladder to the outside of the body, through which urine is released.

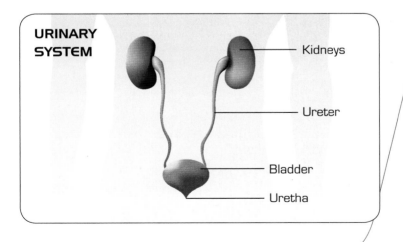

URINARY SYSTEM

Kidneys

Ureter

Bladder

Uretha

CHAPTER SIX

Into the Future

REPRODUCTION IS IMPORTANT for all species of animals, including humans. Much of the body's energy acquisition, protection, waste removal, communication, and movement is aimed at keeping the body healthy for reproduction.

The reproductive system is different in males and females. In males, it is made up of the testes, seminal vesicles, prostate gland, and penis. Two small organs called testes are located inside the scrotum, which is a sac of skin that hangs outside the male's body. The testes produce sperm, which are the male sex cells, and testosterone—the male sex hormone.

Sperm are produced inside tightly coiled tubes within each testis. For sperm cells to develop and survive, they need a temperature a few

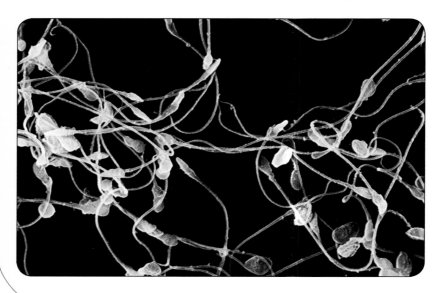

Human sperm magnified 600 times

MALE REPRODUCTIVE SYSTEM

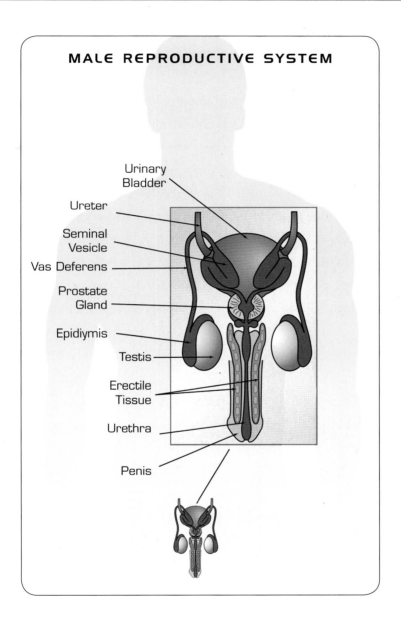

Urinary Bladder

Ureter

Seminal Vesicle

Vas Deferens

Prostate Gland

Epidiymis

Testis

Erectile Tissue

Urethra

Penis

degrees lower than the rest of the body. That is why the scrotum is located outside the body.

When sperm are almost mature, they move into the epididymis and a single larger tube called the vas deferens. They slowly move through the vas deferens, waiting to be released from the body. Saclike structures called seminal vesicles produce a fluid that nourishes the sperm. After the prostate gland adds another fluid that allows that sperm to swim, the mixture of fluids—semen—is released through the penis

In females, the reproductive system is a little more complicated because it is where a fetus develops until it is born. The main female reproductive organs are the ovaries, fallopian tubes, and uterus. Unlike males, who produce sperm after puberty, all of a woman's eggs are developed before she is born. They wait, not quite ready to be fertilized, in the ovaries. Once she reaches puberty, the woman usually releases one egg per month from an ovary. Once released, the egg travels down the fallopian tube toward the uterus. The egg will only live for about 24 hours unless a sperm reaches it first.

If the egg does not meet any sperm in the fallopian tube on its way toward the uterus, it dies, and the cycle begins over again the following month. However, if sperm have entered the female's body through the vagina, traveled toward the uterus, and reached the egg, one of them will most likely

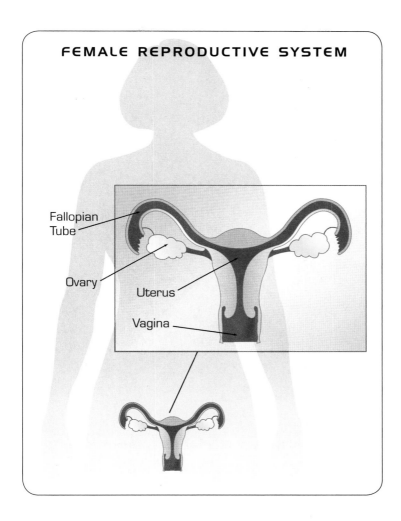

FEMALE REPRODUCTIVE SYSTEM

Fallopian Tube

Ovary

Uterus

Vagina

penetrate the egg's wall and fertilize it.

The united sperm and egg are called a zygote. As a zygote travels through the fallopian tube toward the uterus,

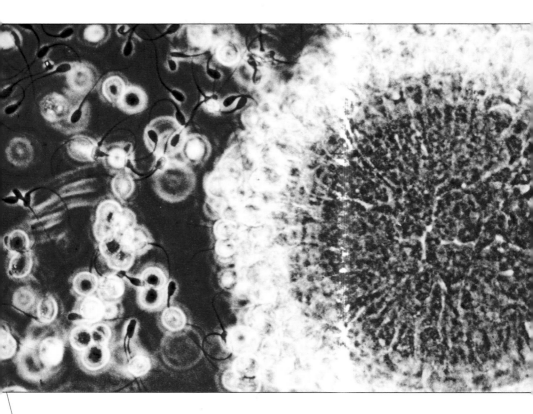

it divides many times until it becomes a hollow ball of cells called a blastocyst. The blastocyst embeds itself in the lining of the uterus about seven to eight days after fertilization. After that, there is a long process until a baby is born. The complete developmental process from fertilization to a baby's birth takes approximately nine months, which is called the gestation period.

A multitude of sperm swarm an egg.

In Vitro Fertilization

Sometimes a couple is unable to have a baby in the usual way. A man may have abnormal sperm, or a woman's eggs may not be released. Over the past 20 years, advances in reproductive medicine have allowed doctors to help these couples. In the process of in vitro fertilization, the woman takes extra hormones to encourage her body to produce multiple mature eggs at one time.

Once they are ready, these eggs are harvested from her body and united with sperm in a small glass dish known as a petri dish. If all goes well, the sperm will fertilize the eggs, forming zygotes that will begin to grow in the dish. After a few days, these zygotes are placed in the woman's uterus, where they can continue their growth normally.

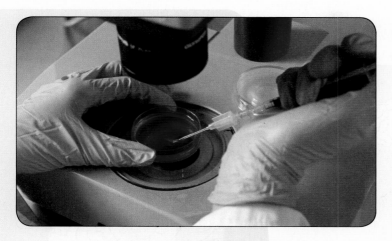

An egg cell is injected with sperm inside a petri dish during in vitro fertilizaton.

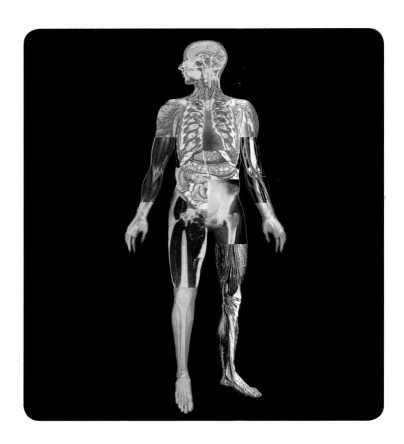

When you perform even simple activities, your body systems are hard at work. Each system has its own function, but each one also depends on the body's other systems. From support and movement to digestion and reproduction, the body's systems work together to keep your body functioning smoothly.

The human body's many systems make up an efficient, living network.

alveoli—tiny sacs in the lungs where blood exchanges carbon dioxide for oxygen

antibodies—special proteins produced by the immune system to fight a particular disease

anus—the opening through which solid waste leaves the body

brain stem—the part of the brain that controls involuntary processes

cerebellum—the part of the brain that coordinates movement

cerebrum—the main part of the brain that controls voluntary processes and interprets information gathered from senses

enzymes—special proteins that start or speed up chemical reactions, such as digestion, in the body

fetus—a developing baby while inside a woman

glands—organs in the body that produce hormones

neurons—specialized cells that transmit impulses in the nervous system

plasma—the liquid part of the blood that carries red blood cells, white blood cells, and platelets

platelets—the part of the blood that helps with clotting after an injury

puberty—the time when boys and girls first become able to reproduce; this occurs at about the age of 14 for boys and the age of 12 for girls

sternum—the breastbone, or large central bone where the ribs attach

vertebrae—the small bones that surround and protect the spinal cord

▹ The average adult male has 11½ pints (5.5 liters) of blood in his body, and the average adult female has 10 pints (4.7 liters). Blood makes up about 7 percent of a person's total body weight.

▹ You can increase the strength of your muscles by doing certain types of exercise, such as weight lifting, on a regular basis. Exercise makes the muscle fibers thicker, which makes them stronger.

▹ Some people are born without any melanin. Other people's bodies are unable to use melanin properly. People in both cases have extremely pale skin, hair, and eyes. This condition is called albinism.

▹ The human brain contains about 100 billion neurons.

▹ The longest cells in the human body are motor neurons. They can be up to 3⅓ feet (1 m) long.

▹ Up to 50 percent of your body heat escapes through your head because of the extensive network of blood vessels close to the skin of your head.

▹ Skin becomes wrinkled in the bathtub because the outer layer of dead cells absorbs water. That outer layer is closely attached to the living layer right underneath, so to make up for the increased surface area, the skin wrinkles.

▹ Skin is the largest organ of the body and makes up 7 percent of body weight.

▹ Women are four times as likely as men to develop osteoporosis.

▹ The cerebrum of the human brain is much larger and more complex than those of animals.

An albino gray squirrel can be easily identified by its white fur and red eyes.

At the Library

Cassan, A. *Introduction to the Human Body.* Philadelphia: Chelsea House, 2006.

Fullick, Ann. *The Human Body.* Des Plaines, Ill.: Heinemann Library, 1999.

Gold, Martha V. *The Nervous System.* Berkeley Heights, N.J.: Enslow, 2004.

On the Web

For more information on this topic, use Facthound.
1. Go to *www.facthound.com*
2. Type in this book ID: 0756519586
3. Click on the *Fetch It* button.
FactHound will find the best Web sites for you.

On the Road

The Franklin Institute
Building 810
Denver Federal Center
Lakewood, CO 80215
303/202-4830

Chicago Museum of Science and Industry
57th Street and
Lake Shore Drive
Chicago, IL 60637
773/684-1414

Explore all the Life Science books

Animal Cells: The Smallest Units of Life

DNA: The Master Molecule of Life

Genetics: A Living Blueprint

Human Body Systems: Maintaining the Body's Functions

Major Organs: Sustaining Life

Plant Cells: The Building Blocks of Plants

A complete list of Exploring Science titles is available on our Web site: *www.compasspointbooks.com*

airways, 27
alveoli, 27, 28–29
antibodies, 29, 30, 35
anus, 33, 37
appendicular skeleton, 9
arteries, 23–24, 25
arterioles, 23, 24
axial skeleton, 8–9

blood donations, 26
blood pressure, 25
blood types, 26
blood vessels,
    7, 8, 23, 25
brain, 5, 13, 15, 16–17,
    19, 20, 21, 22
brain stem, 16–17, 19
bronchi, 27
bronchioles, 27

calcium, 11, 12, 35
capillaries, 23, 24
carbohydrates, 35
carbon dioxide, 5, 24,
    27, 28
cardiac muscles, 13, 14
cartilage, 11
central nervous system,
    16
cerebellum, 16, 17, 19
cerebrum, 16, 17–18
chyme, 34, 36
cilia, 27
circulatory system, 4,
    5, 11, 23–25, 27,
    30, 33

dermis, 6, 7
diaphragm, 27, 28
digestive system, 4–5,
    13, 33–34, 36–37
digestive system
    diagram, 34

eardrum, 20
eggs, 40–42, 43
endocrine system, 4,
    21–22
epidermis, 6, 7
epididymis, 40
esophagus, 34
estrogen, 22

fallopian tubes, 40, 41
fats, 35
frontal lobes, 17, 19

heart, 5, 14, 23, 24, 25

hormones, 22, 35, 43
hypothalamus, 22

immune system, 4,
    29–31
in vitro fertilization, 43
inner ear, 20
interneurons, 15, 16

Jenner, Edward, 32
joints, 11

keratin, 6
kidneys, 37

large intestine, 36
ligaments, 11
lungs, 16, 24, 27, 28

marrow, 11
melanin, 7
microbes, 8, 29, 30
middle ear, 20
minerals, 35
motor neurons, 15, 16
muscular system, 4, 5,
    6, 13–14

nervous system, 4, 5, 7,
    15–18, 20–21, 35
neurons, 15
nutrients, 23, 24,
    35, 36, 37

occipital lobes, 17, 18
osteoporosis, 12
ovaries, 40
oxygen, 5, 23, 24,
    27–28, 29, 35

parietal lobes, 17–18, 19
penis, 38, 40
peripheral nervous
    system, 16
pharynx, 34
pituitary gland, 22
plasma, 23
platelets, 11, 23
pulse, 25

red blood cells, 11, 23,
    35
reproductive system, 4,
    13, 38, 40–42
reproductive system
    diagrams, 39, 41
respiratory system, 4, 5,
    13, 27–29

respiratory system
    diagram, 28
retina, 21
ribs, 9, 28

saliva, 29, 33
scrotum, 38, 40
sense receptors, 21
senses, 15, 17, 20–21
sensory neurons, 15–16
skeletal muscles, 13, 14
skeletal system, 4, 5, 6,
    8–9, 11, 12
skeletal system diagram,
    10
skin, 4, 5, 6–8, 20–21,
    29
skull, 9, 11
small intestine, 34
smooth muscle, 13, 34
sound diagram, 20
sperm, 38, 40–42, 43
spinal cord, 9, 15, 16
sternum, 9
stomach, 16, 34

temporal lobes, 17, 18,
    19
tendons, 14
testes, 38
testosterone, 22, 38
tissues, 9, 21, 24
trachea, 27

ureters, 37
urethra, 37
urinary bladder, 37
urinary system, 4, 13,
    37
urinary system diagram,
    37
uterus, 40, 41, 42, 43

vaccines, 30–31, 32
vagina, 40
vas deferens, 40
veins, 23, 24
venules, 23, 24
vertebrae, 9
villi, 36
vitamins, 35
voluntary muscles, 14

water, 35
white blood cells, 11,
    23, 29–30

zygotes, 41, 43